Me, You, Then Snow

Khashayar Mohammadi

Copyright © 2021 Khashayar Mohammadi

All rights reserved. No part of this work may be reproduced or used in any form, except brief passages in reviews, without prior written permission of the publisher.

Edited by Shane Neilson
Cover and book design by Jeremy Luke Hill
Proofreading by Carol Dilworth
Set in Goudy Old Style
Printed on Mohawk Via Felt
Printed and bound by Arkay Design & Print

LIBRARY AND ARCHIVES CANADA CATALOGUING IN PUBLICATION

Title: Me, you, then snow / Khashayar Mohammadi.
Names: Mohammadi, Khashayar, 1994-
Description: Poems.
Identifiers: Canadiana (print) 20200372874 | Canadiana (ebook) 20200372971 | ISBN 9781774220146 (softcover) | ISBN 9781774220153 (PDF) | ISBN 9781774220160 (EPUB)
Classification: LCC PS8626.O4469 M42 2021 | DDC C811/.6—dc23

ONTARIO ARTS COUNCIL
CONSEIL DES ARTS DE L'ONTARIO
an Ontario government agency
un organisme du gouvernement de l'Ontario

Gordon Hill Press gratefully acknowledges the support of the Ontario Arts Council.

Gordon Hill Press respectfully acknowledges the ancestral homelands of the Attawandaron, Anishinaabe, Haudenosaunee, and Métis Peoples, and recognizes that we are situated on Treaty 3 territory, the traditional territory of Mississaugas of the Credit First Nation.

Gordon Hill Press also recognizes and supports the diverse persons who make up its community, regardless of race, age, culture, ability, ethnicity, nationality, gender identity and expression, sexual orientation, marital status, religious affiliation, and socioeconomic status.

Gordon Hill Press
130 Dublin Street North
Guelph, Ontario, Canada
N1H 4N4
www.gordonhillpress.com

"Alas! who was the third one weeping? I thought we were only two."
—Hossein Panahi

Table of Contents

Moes' Skin	1
Dear Kestrel	9
Salon	23
In Loving Memory of Midnight	49
Homohymns	67

Moes' Skin

1.

Close your eyes. Picture your ego and draw.

A blue whale? A deep trail? Roots.

>   Lover's kiss and mother's bones
>   Fickle thoughts   reminiscent
>   Last oyster uncleft

Close your eyes. Picture my heart and draw.

A cave? Pebble-dashed. Roots.

Each pebble cast into encircling lakes.
Each ripple unfolds into you.

2.

A candle-lit buddha smiled at our cheap incense sticks. Lost in boredom, we spoke ill of the sunrise.

A tame moment of compassion morphed into a wolf pack in your eye. I stretched for your smile, but you balled up into a mountain. Reciting premeditated thoughts of comfort, I ran out of words.

My head cradled sunlight to its resting place. Did you ever have a face?

Erect I backed up into the woods
and your body gathered snow

Erect I danced waterfalls
and your spine sweat arctic winds

A candle-lit buddha smiled at our cheap incense sticks. Lost in boredom, we spoke ill of the sunrise.

A tame moment of compassion morphed into a whale song in your eye. We held hands at the lee, but the waves crushed us into diamonds. Reciting premeditated thoughts of comfort, we ran out of words.

Erect I danced the buddha
and your eyes bled Aurora Borealis

Erect I danced the Adhan
and you slept through forest fires.

A candle-lit buddha smiled at our cheap incense sticks. Lost in boredom, we spoke ill of the sunrise.

Your eye bled incarnations, drunk driving to stitched-up eternities. We sipped each other's tongues in thirst, nose-kissing to epiphany. I peeled you off into a constellation and rode you to my true north.

A candlelit buddha smiled at my reflection. Lost in the boredom of arrival, I spoke ill of you.

3.

Crack of dawn
the morning breeze carries
the malaise of secret kisses.

Nightbus glances glide
past this heavy shell of "I".

Roadside hesitation:
indigo fogs the irreversible.

What you know best becomes a house,
what you know least becomes a road.

Solace in a thought: my brain buttered to asphalt, the coward's refuge.

4.

Pillow's kiss past midnight's stroke and doze down the fugue of highway tunes. Up up and away, past mall-lit windows displaying bootleg DVDs and Ciderhouse blues where hatred blossoms in plastic-bagged opacity. Past the hooka-smoking girls eyeing lustful men in blue.

Felt like a god, but slipped on Moe's Skin.
A new motto for of massage chair afternoons:
>"Don't frown! You'd slip."

A single leaf behind an iPod case;
a Djinn in each passing eccentricity.
I flew back to where the water poured:

> *From up here all is bright; neon dots splashed against god-stricken shacks, shackled. Fluttering glitter, dashing along the five-lane Serengeti. Highway windows hold Mystery men of Blue, half-knit to cascading lace curtains, puffing away exhausted cigarette smoke. Purring cars bow to laundromats; an exhibition of teenage mothers freckled with nocturnal blues. Yanking shirts and slamming doors: another bed left unshared.*

I fly back to trace
our blasphemous steps.
My back to blinding sun
I smiled a masculine smile.
Ticker-taped by rain we strode,
counting down to the promised flood:
>two boys dipped in the absurd;
>two mystery men in blue.

Dear Kestrel

1.

Dear Kestrel,

You dust the evening sun off your shoulders
and ball up on your mattress   aching

Another one of those days...
it's been another one of those days every day for months
passersby may lack compassion
but a hot meal never lies

You're aching, and while aching
you promise yourself you'll be beautiful forever

It's their eyes, Kes
that glance that makes you feel unattractive
fetishized, othered

You avoid eyes by dancing in solitude

Do you feel the weight of your lips, Kes
heavy with withheld proclamations?

You spent spring strolling through cemeteries
searching for the odd cherub to cool your cheek against

and when your lovers leave you can't stand the silence of goodbye

It's the banality of goodbye
It's the static of Sunday gently scratching your soul

and on the subway ride home
comedy happens to ya

You feel the crowd, pulsating to the caress of fading witticisms
anger inspires ecstatic laughter
unintentional/induced   applauded/reproduced

Comedy happens to ya, Kes
laughter the medicine
         the fraternal
         the eternal

2.

For B.D.M.

Dear Kestrel,

In your breast-full hugs: a thought
of unhuggable parents,
of high school girls lining up for lines

Your cheeks don't even allow for a smile to fully blossom,
trust, molested out of your aquiline visage.
Your trembling fingers clutch the pint
harder than they clutch the unwinding strands of childhood

Your impotent lover gets his kicks
outta watching your hips click in and out of balance
and drowning in foster care.
You scrape up that senile delusion and call him "Daddy"
On his chest
the misspelled name of a mother,
her plight for a softer pounding, slammed behind the bedroom door.
And here you are again! Begging "Harder! Harder!"
to feel mother flow in your veins

In post-coital haze, you toddle along the streets
looking for the man who shouts: *"Childhood for sale, only ten bucks a hit"*

3.

Dear Kestrel,

The weirdo bumps into us,
swirls in a methamphetamine haze
and jostles back into the crowd   hardly blending

We float into the night
past singing drunkards and Jesus salesmen
into the intimacy of backalleys and streetcorner loot
      textbooks
      mirrors
      drawers
      loose hangers
      and those one-off sofas you can't imagine
      ever furnished a house
      let alone a home

You found a mattress Kes
with BEDBUGS!!! spraypainted all over,
hurled yourself onto it
and slapped your hand on the emptiness beside

We're the only sober ones for miles
every bollard's found a drunk Kes
couples stage-lit by limping streetlights

but in sobriety we can hear high heels click
above the buzz of the laundromat's neon sign

Lately
each affinity becomes love
moistens to lucidity
prosthetic
to the body
the comradery of stale breath
on a lovers' shoulder

With a limp hug we said goodbye
and I imagined you barefoot
almost floating
tonight I can't sleep Kes
I walk through the back alleys
looking for you, thinking
who were you looking for that night?

4.

Dear Kestrel,

It's the subtle things about Montreal
how loudly people gasp if you dare to cross on red
yet here I am
sitting window-side
watchin' Hasidic Jews glide past in uniform

I sit in silence
daydreaming in broken French

Dear Kestrel,
will I be tragic?
Will I embody enough paradoxes to be beautiful?

I smell death Kes
mothballs chase me wherever I go—
the bedbug smears on the wall Kes
they remind me of you
I stare at the clock
realize how little time has passed...

Dear Kestrel,
last night I saw a little girl
draggin' a toy truck
tethered to her wrist

Was that a poem Kes?
Is this?

Dear Kestrel,
next time don't hesitate
just write

Dear Kestrel,
here's a flower

5.

After Wong Kar Wai

Dear Kestrel,

A few pints in
the pub plays your favorite song
and the alcohol eats away   corroding
a face once loved   stagnant
hovering midway between
          "Shoulda never" & "Coulda once"

In past midnight hues of neon
I can hardly see you Kes

A memory blurred
into a city blurred
without my glasses

throbbing
with a drunken truth binge

without glasses
each light blossoms   gently floating

Rain sweeps solitude into pubs
as if raindrops can probe into amberthickened skin

the clamour
kitchen clangour
filtered through waterfalls:

                    to each a Kestrel of their own

6.

Dear Kestrel,

I look back at the footprints in the sand
look ahead at the ocean   and dive
head first
my arms piercing the horizon line

I'm mirrored
torn at the surface
protruding limbs: the lowest of the horizon
submerged limbs: the highest of the upside down

Dear Kes,
please don't laugh when I say
that I felt a Freudian longing for the womb underwater
that I understood the primacy of all cosmic egg ontologies

Dear Kes,
if I said I'm buoyant
how much would you care
on a scale of hope to anxiety?

I swim aimlessly
waiting for god to seep up my pores
and nestle in a juicy cyst

Dear Kestrel,
I've swam too far
the coast has become but a spec
please send your next message in a bottle

7.

Dear Kestrel,

Sit here a while
sit here with me in candlelight
right by the fiddler
singin' of the Mississippi

The candle's dying light
reflects off your glass of wine
three red streaks on your wrist
what morbid fortune-telling

We watch yarmulke friendships form
amidst an upright bass solo

Dear Kes,
don't call me a miser
just for being five pints in
I've made genuine connections with the world,
found Rilke verses to purify ourselves with

Dear Kestrel,
I keep writing my name on the cocktail napkin
my real name that is
the one that's hard to pronounce
the one that's been mythologized
the one being whispered behind my back

I've lost myself Kes
please come identify me from the lineup

8.

Dear Kestrel,

Fingers clawing your hair
like I'm holding a Hamlet skull
I'm trying to remember you

Kes,
don't you know I'm a solipsism sommelier?
That I do Cartesian meditations before sleep?
That I've got my 2+2=5 demon tatted on my shoulder?
His thought bubble spells your name...

Holding you I know
your pen callus is the sexiest thing about you
we're too pumped full of Go-Pro visions of Zion to read
so we dine to soft erotica
where cleavage is left uncleft

At Costco you asked me to look at the books next to the crop-tops
and I wondered if Moby Dick ever made it to a haberdashery or something

9.

Dear Kestrel,

Holding you I'm prosthetic
holding you I'm the loneliest me
I'll be in the frozen food aisle
let's rendezvous on the other side

Salon

Maybe

After Robert Flanagan's "Why?"

Maybe I don't like war
Maybe I don't like being the one who speaks against war
Maybe I don't like those who criticize those who speak against war
Maybe I don't like those who understand those who criticize those
    who speak against war
Maybe I don't like those who defend those who understand those who
    criticize those who speak against war
Maybe I don't like those who hate those who defend those who
    understand those who criticize those who speak against war
Maybe I don't like being relatable…

Maybe I hate being relatable so much I'm relatable
Maybe I don't trust myself…

Maybe I love myself
Maybe I love myself so much I seek podiums to yell "I love myself"
Maybe I love myself so much I criticize those whose pain is not trendy
    enough for them to seek podiums to yell "I love myself"

Maybe I'm worth it, even without sapphire hair dye
Maybe I'm worth it, even without turquoise lipstick
Maybe I'm right
Maybe I'm right so often I'm farther right than I thought I was…

Maybe I love liberty so much I applaud
Maybe I love liberty so much I suffocate
Maybe I love liberty so much that once upon a time I yelled at a man
    who trusted his senses
Maybe senses are all we've got…

Maybe words are outdated
Maybe speech is so archaic we're borderline metaphysical
Maybe grouping nouns together is so problematic we're already
    ethereal
Maybe next time I wanna call you I have to vibrate at your frequency,
    molecule by molecule

Maybe this is Poetry
Maybe if I said this was Poetry you would laugh more

Maybe whatever mate it doesn't even fucking matter
Maybe I respectfully disagree
Maybe I understand but there's nothing I can do
Maybe there's no reason to raise your voice sir
Maybe...

Maybe this is the beginning of Poetry
Maybe soon enough we'll all gather in groups to listen in silence, lost
    for words
Maybe *"Spare the rod and spoil the child"*
Maybe *"You always hurt the one you love"*

Clumsy Hunters

"Words are clumsy hunters of the truth" — *Metin Kahraman*

an accident
"unprecedented…"

foot-soles
aching from "anxiety"

smiles exchanged in the Hospital cafeteria

a "lack"
flesh-woven

a "void"
midnight-hued

her fluorescent farewell
"ticking" into ephemera

one "last" heartbeat

shit-soiled sheets
carried off by the "Nurse"

vending machines
humming to the "grief"-struck

a "solitude"
trapped in a lover's arms

a "warmth"
sweeping plastic bags across the road

a "silence"
for impermanence

***

the carbon monoxide you "breathe" in the tunnel

the tongue
pressed against your teeth in repressed "anger"

the love you "deny" yourself
the love you "bargain" for

the black cloth
measured to "elegantly" cup genitals for a funeral

the generic pop-song
rudely interrupting your "memories"

eviscerated closets
bruised eyes
cracked mugs
unsaid "goodbyes"

***

a winter
spent on the "self"

"sobriety"
chipped into pockets

burnt "bridges"
and
slammed doors

a silver spoon
dizzy from stirring
"sugarless!"

You are "fearless"
You are "healthy"
You are "whole"

Job's done
why don't you just go "home?"

                                          ***

bokeh
dancing dust
streetlight tracers
"12th step" hasn't come

"Insecure"?
love reeks of "acceptance"
no more "bargaining"

only "Truth"
night-bus glances
humans to-be

Sungai Buloh

For Agnes Ong

Shouldered a burden
To the depth of the jungle
Boots licked clean
By the hem of nature's garments
Rattling hello to feet
That never trod on pristine land

Our ride leaves
Exhaust smoke
Cloud-spelling
    Eight hours till your electronics faint!

In the Kampung
You're as visible as the brightest star
In the Kampung
"Revelation" means a Durian
"Redemption", an awaited downpour
Apocalyptic thunderstorms
Trees kowtow till broken

And before long
The embrace of a temple
Joss-sticks thicker than my thumb

Highway isn't far but tonight
We're the darkness behind those trees

this poem wears your clothes, sleeps in your bed, but is not, in fact, you

For Terese Mason Pierre

                    kissed
under the throbbing veins
of this city
            for once
    living out loud

      surrounded
by bronchial hues
of Capitalism
our bodies
entwine
into a slip knot:
             tears shed
over fulfilled wishes

'*ride or die*'
astrology made witness
            /a wishbone cracks
and I don't dare look

      out of concrete
     we surface
    afternoon sun
   cradling your natural geometry:
         Venus-in-fur nostalgia

              baring scars
             you ask me
"do lilacs yearn for their root family?"
"Purple white ink in Earth?"
and with a glass of wine
I paint you
onto the neighbour's "Garage Sale!" sign

you're unravelling
holding you I unlearn object permanence
                step in front of the mirror
                    wash my face for you
                    down the drain it goes

Schrader's "First Reformed"

Where were you when I laid the Earth's foundation?

Unsure. But we'll be here
to witness it crumble.
Will you ever forgive us?

The desert of the real
is a mouse click away.
Don't just watch and contemplate.
Crack turns schism,
salt to melt all winters away

Where were you when I laid the Earth's foundation? you ask
and I reply, *Where will you be when Noah comes back?*

Haneke's "Code Unknown"

it begins with innocence
a shadow approaches a wall
torn from its body
the trajectory of individualism

at a distance
fate appears opaque
only understood in fragments

and escape:
once as roaring, as fireworks
once as sneaking, as culture
once as candid, as a lingering glance

The Farewell

For Khusro Mohammadi

"More tears are shed over answered prayers than unanswered ones."
— Truman Capote

the bird by grandma's window
trembles with familiar frailty
hers is the 451st window from the highway
the 11th from the sewage canal
where pest control has given up

she sits by the window day and night
and when the neighbour brings home a lover
her eyes glide over their young bodies
and settles under the mulberry tree
where the airport taxi parked years ago

aunty calls: grandpa's dying
uncle calls: grandpa's dying
grandma calls: grandpa's lying down
lulled into youth by the hum of radio older than me

each time family calls
(each time we share LED smiles
and audio-delayed excuses)
affection disrupts distance
          -oh wait-
distance disrupts affection

Dad's voice is only happy
when on the phone with home
when speaking Farsi
when there's family around
and there never seems to be

on weekends
Dad travels a couple hours
to rent the scent of home for another week
to stand in long lines to buy meat butchered
by someone familiar to his longing

at home
Dad speaks of cultural differences
of Canada's marvellous education
and its inefficient electricians
of its clean air and expensive housing

Mom's lost in images
spends her days staring into screens
from Skype to CRA web forms
to Netflix to Candy Crush

"Have we done the right thing?"
finds its answer in a generation or two
when death cleaves culture
into its geographically destined borders

from grandfather's eyes: a memory
a stubborn boy stands by his bed
and refuses to sleep

grandpa says
"Go to bed"
and the boy goes
and stands on his bed

grandpa says
"Go to sleep"
and the boy closes his eyes while standing

the boy does everything grandpa says
exactly as he describes it, Word, by word
and he defies till grandpa knows what he desires
Word, by word

each breath is a countdown
and I'm careful what I wish for these days
since life reminds me of that stubborn little boy

Tarkovksy's "The Sacrifice"

What does death think
of an aesthetic education?
What can philosophy do
to extinction?

Behind the camera
The aging artist
is faced with death.
The Television foretells tragedy.
The housewife is histrionic, inconsolable.

Under the male gaze:
she must be sedated
into apathy

A house
by a puddle
by a house
by a lake
by a house
in the ocean.

Microcosm,
or synecdoche?

A sacrifice has been made
and the artist lives!
"Eternal recurrence"
he says.

Pornhub Podcast with Asa Akira and Brooke Candy

"I do have a dash of Kramer in me" – Brooke Candy

So no sex in high school eh?
Your dad workin' in *Hustler* and all,
Larry Flynt at your brother's bar mitzvah
so you snuck around

but
Pornhub's got you now
making queer porn and all
no "normal sex" you say
as in no straight men
the universe budding
from a bejeweled asshole
hugs and butterflies
the screen flashes
CUM NOW
and genitals are constellated
rudimentary CGI

Asa says
we've all got daddy issues
is that why we're hypersexual?

Courtney Love's been tame for ages
Anna Nicole's gone
your sex is your weapon now
your pictures flagged every other day
popping in and out of public consciousness
Trojan-horsing gender identity issues into pop culture
making queerness punk again
making punk queer again

queer as in suck you
in the bathroom
and then slide you
and your eccentric beauties a pill
for the cuddle pile

queer as in 45% dislikes
queer as in "I'll pass on this"
queer as in "the lighting is all wrong"
queer as in "stale in its sameness"
queer as in "visual unclarity"
queer as in "the adult film industry lacks beauty"
queer as in NOT FOR STRAIGHT MEN

Bergman's "Through a Glass Darkly"

nightmares
of wolves who bare their teeth
an allegory of disease perhaps

Faroese twilight
brings out the sincerity
of the ocean

gulls nest
in the attic crawl space
where walls give way
like foliage
where she became a chorus
promising God's return to man
creativity
is the death drive in motion
and libido in stalemate
it's man's final tool for survival

untethering the boat on the jetty:
    a promise of rain

the chorus sings once again
walls turned foliage
light reflected and refracted through water
a single moment of disbelief
and we've all aged visibly

"Walk quietly"
God will soon be among us
will soon walk through that door

a flash of light
bouncing off the ocean surface
and through the window

Bergman's "Persona"

the actress on stage
a writer's tool for empathy
she sharpens her eyes
to balance the softness
of her face

she decides not to speak,
but to dive

music invades, dresses thoughts in armour

the television shows a burning monk
and the actress recoils in horror
refusal to speak
to participate
to become a broken cog
white and black
black and white
long hair / short hair
mute, talkative
nursing, or be nursed
studying, or be studied

the self we see
mirrored on screen quarantined by a silver curtain

to see oneself in the actress
is to make a leap of faith
a cultural martyrdom
of imagery

the actress,
once muted,
becomes an empty vessel
to be projected onto
the actress in doubt
performing femininity

as the camera zooms in
the quarantine is lifted
the self is at arm's length
in the eyes of the actress

Haneke's "The Piano Teacher"

to lose oneself
to the pupil
and to know one is lost
in the process

to give oneself up

music is a lot less descriptive
than we think
music can wake the heart
but what is the music?

to the pupil
the music
is heart mathematics
a sonata, if well performed,
can color one's desire

a Piano:
mechanical Passion
for the unrequited

Aronofsky's "Mother!"

in the case of a fire, abandon your loved one. keep your body firmly aching at all times. should they put up a fight, a soft "I love you" shall inspire consent. the heart may desire more firewood, so look them in the eyes. remember: you may feel the weight of your teeth weighing down your skull. you may look down and find your feet firmly planted in ash. you may experience mild discomfort. you might feel the urge to take the weight off your feet; that desire, however prevalent, must be oppressed at first. wiggle your toes and lift your feet slowly: cinders of a loved one, crystallized into a mirror. open your eyes and gaze at the eyes staring back. moisten your lips, open your mouth and whisper "I love you" again to reacquire consent.

Tarkovsky's "The Mirror"

For Claudia Edwards

cum-throes of a cock
death-throes of a bird
trapped in a fist
and the skin
that sheathes our soul opaque

a dried leaf
in the pages of history
blighted
once green

Sun and Steel

for Yukio Mishima

Sun:

soothes the skin
warm and literal

Sun:

holds earth
holds us
holds death

Sun:

does not blossom
unless bled

Sun:

shaped
into daggers
piercing

Sun:

once bled
can nurture
bodies

Sun:

needed
for departure

Sun:

meets steel
shines dutifully

Steel:

shaping
or to be shaped

Steel:

is death
the eloquence
of instrument?

Steel:

can make
that body bleed

Steel:

shaped
into light

Steel:

once shaped
can nurture minds

Steel:

the wheel
the road
the map

Steel:

finishes
what sun started

In Loving Memory of Midnight

The Orange Pool Noodle

Feels like the first time
skin   abstracted
into music

"when in doubt
carve your feelings
into wood"

All winter, I
chipped sobriety onto the floor
as embryonic dreams
auditioned in the dark

But my mind
sat on the throne
pulling a lever
and to the crocodiles they went

Vancouver

this stillness

logs lined up
on the beach

the more I say
the more I take
from this city

listen
~~~~~~~~

the rhythm of the waves
~~~~~~~~

I froth at the mouth
imitating the ocean

where I don't belong
is full of waiting
hours spent
hitching rides
on strangers' lashes

open my mouth
my tongue turns to sand

open my eyes
my feet turn to stone

Nipples Al Dente

Scars say
        "The End's a dreadful thought"

in the cross-legged hours to come
be more masculine

bitemarks embolden   heavy as lips
bus-ride boredom taught us
how to forget the word "longing"
how to say "I" and really mean it this time
how to bite
        anti-oedipal
        complex free

we paved a new path to the mind
found immaternal love protruding

my skin came alive
a fingertip could stretch me tender
etch a lover's mark on hips

chest-risen
        exorcised
                a warmth permeates

        We're Longing-Free!

Ode to Mr. Churchyard

After Søren Kierkegaard

think dusk, think lake, think indigo.
think thistles rattling so loud the wind runs away in stitches.

electricity gallops on transmission towers,
hilltops glance at urban life.

stand in silence and ache for thawed recollections of childhood.
bokeh of floating traffic lights: second-hand nostalgia, VHS induced.

with the last ray of sunset your shadow climbs back into its vessel.
cool breeze to color in that silence:

an echo
of   an echo
of   an echo
of   an echo

The Pencil Sharpener

For Simon Wilner

woodchips in the basin
the dog's swallowed a piece and pierced his stomach

winter's knocking
on the workshop door
a storm's brewing

and the earth and I've got a minute
till our embrace becomes fatal

woodchips in the basin
the dog's swallowed a piece and pierced his stomach

Canada Day 2019

I stare down at the blade
a knife
cleaves and separates
fruit from seed
flesh from
skin, ligament
bone, muscle, silverskin

I place it on my fingertip
and press firmly till it bleeds open
slides away like a torn glove
tucked into the pocket
kept secret

a single projectile
neon blood
against the night sky

slicing
bleeding
dripping

gone

Greg's goodbye party

it was the last party
at the dingy apartment above the Parkdale taverna

you and I tied as "best noses of the party"
that tall girl came in a close third
we answered her questions like
                "where you from?
and   "why have young people abandoned Rock music?"

I necked two litres of Ontario wine
sauntered around the place
begging people to punch me

we stepped on the rooftop
and Greg's muscular friend
flashed us his 8 pack
he was cirque du soleil
I asked him for a punch
and he delivered
right in the abdomen

I cried from joy
came lucid from pain
the pain strong enough for me to clog and unclog a toilet

[pause]

static crawling up and down. no signal.
jump-cut to you yanking me off the rooftop ledge
death gleaming in your eyes
                you screamed "What where you thinking?"

and I fell silent
I've been thinking of Houdini all the while

Pastoral

stepped onto the train
with my death foretold by a friend
a death more imminent than before

the train window: a kaleidoscope
Canadian pastoral
and in a tall wheat field
I retrieved my childhood

Dad's car traveling up north
slithering along mountain roads
and the jokes he told

once I watched a film
about a father-son roadtrip
the father told jokes
just like mine
there was an accident
which left the father
looming above
his son's limp body
told to pull the plug

after that film
Dad's road jokes made me cry
bet he never understood why

I remember...
I remember so much:

my loyal travel companion:
the little boy I imagined
jumping acrobatically
passing obstacles low and tall

my books
which I read stubbornly
nauseous like mother warned

and those quiet moments
on long straight roads
Dad humming to keep his sanity

and the struggle to get some shut-eye
to maybe shave an hour or so off this trip
Mom loved the toll booths
for the merchants selling fresh walnuts
and fruit leather so sour it made your blood sugar drop

Now, here by the Detroit river
I breathe the same humid air
the same small town aspirations
of a better species

walking through the sculpture garden
war is but a nightmare

my footsteps falter
and I stop by a bush
abandoning my solitude
to motorboat lilac blossoms till I'm sated

a gust of wind
a bukkake of cherry blossoms
oh lord! not in my hair

a year ago when Mom asked me
what I loved most about Canada,
I didn't dare say it was the underground
labyrinths leading to washrooms

but today I feel more in love with Canada
than ever before
with trees that mother its pastures
and the ever-present lake [singular]
bleeding its mystique into rivers, ponds, canals

...five more hours to kill
so I sit in a diner
right hand forking scrambled eggs
left hand holding open Rilke
and halfway across the world
from so-called "home"
the Detroit river gulps down my gaze

Soon it'll rain on all the left behind.

Hunger

Constipated thoughts
of teenage insecurity

                                                     How can sugar
                                           remedy wounds of love?

My heart beating
to the refrigerator hum

Mother's gaze
emanates from the chill of the chalk wall

                                                      Is this love?
                                         Or am I hungry again?

No pockets ghazal

long hair as religion, or a Samurai's locks, his honour
I let my beard grow to feel more in tune with my past

restless at dusk, government cruelties
I step out of my shadow and slip into the Blood Moon's robes

dormant on tenement roofs, stretched velvety in tropical exhaustion
tonight we don't have pockets and it inspires children

dismantling highway geometries, waving to the past we've inherited geographically
touch me and I thaw at the tip of your fingers

on the main strip, the neon signs are thinning daily
booksellers gone missing, governments hush hush about it

mirror ventriloquy, I hone my desire to feel more in tune with my past
unibrow beauty   hairy arms beauty

Treefrog

After Nima Youshij

Anxiety
in a jazz-stricken cup

Death-throes
of a flightless bee

—a grain of pollen
mildewed

Once-white lace curtains flail
cherried with soot

Cockroach-ridden shack whose seams
crack in sullen rain-dance screech

Grief-struck and stranded
at the mercy of the treefrog's song

Anemone

For Daniel Renton

When I speak of the body, I speak
of its ability
to reconnect and repair

A finger can be detached, kept in ice
and woven back into existence,
nerve by nerve, re-animated Lovecraft style

The lake is a body without organs.
I am an organ without a body.
My body is a schism between selves.
Each self is a homeland to the body.
So I lay down on the waterfront
to reconnect, extend limbs as an offering
of nautical community housing
and float weightless: an anemone

Soul cum water a la Heraclitus,
lake as bulwark for summer self
and the self-doubt gang

Lake horizon, silver moonlight curving the sky
into M.C. Escher eternities and me at its zenith
flossing cliff sides

Pornhub Gay

For Kirby

the bodies I attract
the bodies I'm attracted to
curves and sinews
muscle symmetry
epidermal glimmer

no body without warmth
no touch void of electricity

the most oppressed bodies
are the most pornographically desired

the most oppressed bodies
are the most pornographically endowed

the most suppressed desires
(of) the most oppressed bodies…

desire
infinitely flexible
bending sexwards
and the oppressed are
the most lusciously bodied
aggressively membered
then dis-membered
dis-embodied
                and re-membered
in taglines

an old, limp dick
hooded with smegma
liver-spotted   sour stench
-the kind that hits you like a fine wine-
unfolds   half-mast
while cultures fuck each other
into self-consuming wormholes

Cyber City

whiskey in wine glasses
cutting the sting
of our cheap cigarettes
philosophizing
with arms suspended
above a heap of cigarette butts

our late-teen minds
scrambling for meaning
in the purple neon
lighting last night's slashed paintings

thirsty for each others' lips
tasting the whiskey
on another's tongue tip
teeth   gnashing into flesh
we gave and withdrew
gave and withdrew
absent eyes on our naked bodies
men bare their canines
behind our eyelids
with every thrust

but it was never about sex
it was about the cigarette we'd share after
the neon corona of a cyber city
dragging us into orbit
humid days when
we'd stare down at striped walkways
so long the first gaze skyward tunneled
clouds into an ever receding sinkhole

we expected to be different after
walk erect as sacrament
buttocks sliding to reveal
where the flame licks clean

chest hair
chest hair
it's all good for now

Homohymns

Homonymic

Man

a hand touched
loved
reclaimed
and withdrawn

                                                             me

and sat across
a cross-legged man

Toe

feet hardened by sand
stretched towards the sun
like beach umbrellas

                                                           you

a man
a toe

Pass

moments *pass* hours
as cars *pass* trucks
on the highway

                                                        then

and once *passed*
become *past*
seemingly still
to the child
at the rear window
waving goodbye

Barf

climbed up
the frozen fire escape
and five shots later
hunched over

                                                  snow

Barf

painting the grey winterscape
with inner greenery

Maw

a hole
gaping

teeth fading
into the void between

                                                  us

man against *maw*

Bar

On the drunkard's shoulder
a *Bar*   open
for business

                                              load

beers   in exchange
for memories
of the unrequited

Two / Be

broken in *two*
longing *to be*
longing

                                                                         in / without

and transcribed
in*to*
grainy photos

midnight
Blue/Red
lens flares

to be
*two be*ings

mad

on the seashore

water   driven *mad*
frothing at the mouth

                                                                   high tide

flossing crabs through rocky teeth

and sat comfortably
on a saline tongue
the two of us

Djineology of Rumi

For Christina Baillie

He knew that he was contending against a Deev, and he put forth all his strength, but the Deev was mightier than he, and overcame him, and crushed him under his hands – from Ferdowsi's "Shahnameh" as translated by Helen Zimmern

Rumi says to leave behind all earthly possessions
to become *Divaneh*
to act like a *Deev*

Deev from *Da'eva*
through Avestan
but *Da'eva* makes *Devil*
through the indo-european connection

Morality at the hands of etymology

Divaneh
now *crazy* from old Swedish *Krasa*
to crush, shatter
jagged edges of a consciousness
once prevalent   now
too sharp to fit into any rounded conversation

but there's a second etymology
that says *Deev* through *Deva*
Deva makes *Divine*

Rumi says "*Divaneh Sho*"
Is it "Become mad!"
or become divine?
To be touched
transcendent
gifted

Deev
now chiefly *Demon*
(through Greek *Daemon*)
originally benevolent
semi-holy
dysphemized by history

crazy
gone back to Persian
becomes *Majnun*
possessed by a *Djinn*
Genius
the Roman appropriation of *Daemon*

e.g.
Socrates had a *Daemon*
Da Vinci had a *Genius*

Djinns promised real
by the *Qur'an*
have become B-movie tropes now

e.g.
young girl moves to rural town
her dorm room is possessed by a *Djinn*

a *Djinn* she can now carry
like a venereal disease
she can become *Djinn-deh*
a "Prostitute"
a *Djinn*-giver

but *Majnun*
is tragic obsession (Love)
Romeo
at the end of his wits
driven to poetry by love
roaming the desert so long
parents have given up hope

Majnun
possessed
fragmented, but whole
in eternal exile
prone to ventriloquy
{often called schizophrenia}
wearing a thick layer of dusk
as eye shadow
and sailing the choppy waters
of taxi window blinds
staring out the window
and into the mind
the sheer effort of existence
scratched onto the spine
roaming the concrete deserts
of indifference
days dictated
by pharmaceuticals

now...
ask me again
about etymology:

Deev <= Da'eva => Devil

or

Deev <= Deva => Divine

The Farewell: Part II

for Khusro Mohammadi

   a blanket
of morning thoughts and snowlight
white on white

news comes of the death
         and I do nothing but think
of filling the fruit bowl for visitors

a city
widowed in the bones of winter
I don't remember boarding the bus
but it's filled with bouquets of flowers
and the boredom of all those holding them

news comes of the death
and I find a new room in my house
new bookshelf   new wallpaper
      was Red always this Red?

news comes of the death
and there's sand on the streetcar again
              where does it come from?
Ash to Ash
Dust to Dust
my thoughts
            caught in a grey sludge

mote of dust
mote of *düst*
snow-motes fall off the *ü*
        düst now dust

news comes of the death
and I find a new corner in the room
with death   I've absorbed new vision
news comes of the death
and I sit silently
wait for the visitors to arrive

"God Gone Astray In The Flesh"

After Frantz Fanon and Douglas R. Hofstadter

my tongue
twisting
into my mother tongue
    entwined
    a new set
of vowels
for this chilly night of
consonants
shrill
       with friction
like piss
 in toilet water

past is lowly
   a place of pasture
past is a dialect
I no longer speak
       fluently
and my present
is hemorrhaging selves

my body
my *tan*
my epidermal S.E.L.F
     aching

I wanna be on my knees
hearing
   "[shut up and] *suck-it*"
and I'll do both

without moaning
the tongue can explore
                  much
much
the tip   disappearing

male for man
male for *tan*
male to be male
the desire to arrive
    [at the *khod*
become *khod-a*
"god" in the flesh
S.E.L.F.-aware]

S.E.L.F.
stands for
S.E.L.F.-Enlightened Life Force
above each S.E.L.F.
An endless ladder
            of S.E.L.(F. /ves)

(-enter THE TORTOISE
with ACHILLES asymptotically
approaching

-ACHILLES: knock knock
-TORTOISE: *Qui est?*
-ACHILLES: *man*
-TORTOISE: *man who?*
-ACHILLES: the *who-man!*
one pillar of the threefold
path, Zarathustra's Nietzsche
travelling west come cover
of dusk)

and taking my eyes
off the L.E.D. corona
of texted nudes
my witching hour sunspots
supernova behind eyelids

the psychedelia
of self-theft
self-*loss*
nebulous in its fragments
fragmented in its piercing light
oozing from eye sockets
onto wrinkled foreheads
                    "Mint in Mortar"

I stare into mirrors
that refuse to reflect
till medication can herd thoughts
       into pasture
            leash all that intrudes
till I'm my own mirror   *khod-a*
S.E.L.F. reflective
till I know clearly that I exist

Odourless Poem

for Bardia Sina'ei

boo is smell
but *boo* is also in *boodan*
which is "to be"

like the phrase
be toe boodan
"to be without you"
but the persian *be*
means without
be toe
"without you"

the *boo* in *boodan*
akin to english Be

to be

but the persian *to*
means "Inside" or "In"
and the persian *In*
means "this"

to be
is illegible
but *be-to*
means "No Insides" or "empty"

to be *be-to*
to be "empty"   "endless"

to be *be-boo*
to be odourless
to be *two* beings
to be into *be-to* beings
people hollowed out
in two
"Right Here"

be toe
be you
without you

longing to *be*-longing
where *loss* is a "flirt"
and *law* is "between"
man and *ma(w)*
but
longing to "no"-longing
to be *into* beings
"right here"
without you
you flirt
you husky *man*
where *man* is "me"
be toe as in *man*
"without you" as in "me"
as in
the crux "of this" translation

be toe man *as in [...]*
a "toe-less" man [fled] "off of this" [sentence]

I is a noise I make without you
instead of "ouch"
notice the "ch" in both
"ouch" and "ache"
like a german "Ich"
but in no way related
we can all proclaim ourselves in pain

I am *man*
an existent "me", aching

as man be toe
"from me to you"
man to toe
me in you
toe be man
you *be* me
you without me

now *share*
this "poem"

share a man
is "my poem"
that I wrote for me
for myself
for *a man*
as man
as you

I = am
flipped to *ma(w)*
this is "Us" now

man　　*toe*　　*ma(w)*
me
you
and our teeth
fading into the void between
man vs ma(w)

teeth
locked into a *jaw*
which is a "place" of its own
in jaw
"this place"
be jaw
"without place"
"exiled?"

man o toe in jaw
"me and you, here"
me and you
connected by an O

add another O
and it becomes OO
third person
genderless

man
o
toe

me
and
you

man
o
toe
o
oo

me
and you
and a third person

genderless [(pro)-]noun

Circumnavigating Heaven in Three Geographies

Parkdale

when B speaks of her drugs
I keep hearing "Heaven"
I sip "Heaven" from my pint of gin
and speak etymologies
say how in Farsi "Heaven"
is simply "Behesht"
akin to English "Best"
how "Heaven" is just us living our best lives
she cuts another line
and walks back into the crowd
her dime bag of coke
rolling onto wet asphalt

and I make a wish
crush it under my feet

Grandma's House

Grandma says Pomegranates are heavenly
that each holds a seed directly from Paradise
and she seeds painstakingly slow
Grandma's no storyteller

one seed rolls onto the carpet
Blue paisley/ Red diamond
and I make a wish
crush it under my feet
and listen to the gentle static
of car tires on wet asphalt
a motorway behind every window

Parkdale

B is gone
days begin with silence
everything in the house faces the lake
where all the light seems to come from

the first ray of sunlight tells me
I can't crawl back into the kitchen
so I coil around myself
stare at the Television I can't turn on
crave a cigarette
stare at the lighter I can't reach
crave a drink
stare at the bottle I can't reach
and sit
stewing
in the soft whisper of car tires
from somewhere behind
everywhere-I've-lived-as-a-child
redeeming everyone-I've-loved-as-a-child
the buzzing silence
like all the afternoon naps I never took
and the five lane motorway
with asphalt crackling
hidden from sight
but ever present
always heard from behind
like the sour breath
breathing dew-drops onto my shoulder blades

I walk onto the balcony
where all light seems to come from
and stare down
and into the lake
and ache
to descend
into my best
Into my "heaven"

Lakeshore

For Kirby

my head
weighing down
my limp body
fingertips searching body parts
I name them with eyes closed
"Nose", "Cheek", "Lip"
one by one
I earn body parts
speak to some for the first time

words embody
and I listen
pen in hand
list myself limb by limb
"Leg", "Leg", "Foot"
gentle swell of "Breast"
larger than most

In winter
the hardest feat is to stand
a body limp from gravity

"Hand", "Leg", "Mouth"
words are arbitrary
but we still use them wrong

It's dangerous
when words stop at sharing
It's dangerous
when words don't inform

and my true form
shaped by words
my true figure
informed by shapes
my true shape
figured out and figured in
formed into a firm corpus
where thoughts flow body in
and life flows body out

bodies elocute louder than words
and we never listen
to limbs who break up
pursue solo careers in expression
while heads sit atop bodies
limp and flaccid

if my skin lies about me
then what of the nights
when all is sour but touch

It's dangerous when words stop at catharsis
and I'm left bare on the bed
asking for a slap
to heat up the skin
so I can surface
to my "Heaven"

Acknowledgements

Great thanks to my partner Terese Pierre for being the light of my life. Thanks to my editor Shane Neilson who sculpted this book into what it is. Thanks to Joseph Ianni and Shima Ra'eesi without whom I'd have never written poetry. Thanks to Kirby for publishing a number of these poems in a chapbook Dear Kestrel. Many thanks to my parents for being supportive. Thanks to countless talented friends who inspire. Thanks to Klara Du Plessis for bringing out the amateur linguist within me. And great thanks to Ali and Tolga, The Brothers Yalcin.